ERIC

Oh No They AREN'T

SCIENCE

ILLUSTRATED BY
SAM CALDWELL

Turn the page
for a science
celebration!

words&pictures

First published in 2025 by words & pictures,
an imprint of The Quarto Group.
100 Cummings Center, Suite 265D
Beverly, MA 01915, USA
T (978) 282-9590 F (978) 283-2742
www.quarto.com

EEA Representation, WTS Tax d.o.o.,
Žanova ulica 3, 4000 Kranj, Slovenia

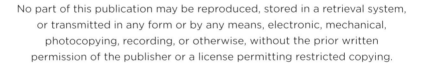

Copyeditor: Nancy Dickmann
Project Editor: Jackie Lui
Designer: Kathryn Davies
Art Director: Sarah Chapman-Suire
Associate Publisher: Holly Willsher
Production Manager: Nikki Ingram

ISBN: 978-0-7112-9281-9

Manufactured in Guangdong, China TT052025

9 8 7 6 5 4 3 2 1

MIX
Paper | Supporting
responsible forestry
FSC® C016973

ERIC HUANG

Oh No They
AREN'T

SCIENCE

FASCINATING
FACTS YOU NEVER
KNEW ABOUT ALL
THINGS SCIENCE!

ILLUSTRATED BY
SAM CALDWELL

words & pictures

CONTENTS

Around the world again?

Our bond is all about chemistry!

I thought this was a wireless TV. . .

I wish we had this book on my planet!

INTRODUCTION

Science is all about figuring out how things work. It means asking questions and conducting experiments to discover and then test possible answers. Science has many different branches, each with a different focus. For example, chemistry explores what things are made of and how they interact, while physics explores how things move and change through time. Geology is the scientific study of the Earth, while astronomy focuses on space.

Science affects every aspect of life, from what you're wearing and what you had for breakfast, to the weather outside. But how much do you really know about science? Everyone knows that liquid water becomes ice when it freezes. **Chemical reactions** are responsible for this. . . aren't they?

The force of **gravity** that keeps planets in our **solar system** from flying off into deep space is the strongest force in the universe, right? Recent changes in Earth's climate are all part of natural processes, and canals spotted on the planet Mars are signs of **extraterrestrial** life. . . aren't they?

OH NO THEY AREN'T!

TURN THE PAGE to find out what you *didn't know* about science!

You'll learn how human activity is causing climate change.

Science clears the air.

You'll find out about different types of engineering that continue to revolutionize the way we live—with some of them also helping to protect the environment.

Science connects the world.

You'll discover chemical reactions, powerful forces of attraction, and the rock-and-roll lifestyle of planet Earth. Through science, you can examine the smallest **atoms** to the largest galaxies—and get to know the universe just a little bit better.

A groundbreaking read!

Look up words in **bold** in the glossary on page 60.

GEOLOGY ROCK AND ROLL

The science of our planet and what it's made of is called geology. Did you know that Earth is over 4.5 billion years old? Imagine the candles on that birthday cake! Things on our planet are pretty much the same as they've always been. . . aren't they?

OH NO THEY AREN'T!

For the first billion years or so, Earth was a hot and hellish ball of rock, covered in volcanoes and bombarded by rocks from space. There were no oceans and almost no atmosphere!

Temperatures cooled about 3.8 billion years ago, and centuries of rainfall followed to cover the planet's surface with water. It would take another billion years before there was enough oxygen for **microscopic** living things to breathe. And hundreds of millions of years before animals could call the planet home.

How much longer do I have to wait?

The Earth has three layers. The top layer, where we live, is called the **crust**. The next layer, called the **mantle**, is made up of very hot rock that can move a little. At the center is the metallic **core**—solid in the middle with a liquid layer surrounding it.

The crust is made up of **tectonic plates** that float on the mantle, like moving puzzle pieces. Every continent, mountain, and ocean sits on top of one or more of these moving pieces.

Luckily, the tectonic plates are no longer rocking and rolling. They're fixed in their locations. . . aren't they?

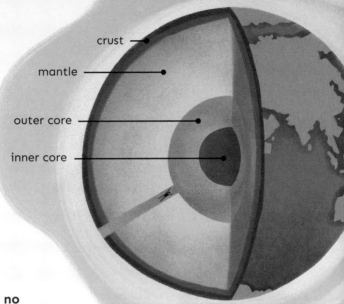

crust

mantle

outer core

inner core

OH NO THEY AREN'T!

Welcome to our continent!

The Himalayas formed when two plates crashed into each other. They're still growing by about 0.2–0.4 inches every year, because the plates are still pushing into each other. Movements between tectonic plates also cause earthquakes and volcanoes.

Guess I'll have to swim the long way round. . .

All this moving means that a map of ancient Earth wouldn't look familiar at all. And if you can wait a billion years or so, you might be able to shake hands with friends and family across the ocean!

HARD ROCK

The building blocks of rocks are called minerals. A mineral is a solid, non-living natural substance with a regular internal structure. Gold is a mineral. So is salt. Some minerals, such as diamonds, contain only one type of mineral. Others, like granite, are a mix of different minerals.

Rocks are divided into three main types: **igneous**, **sedimentary**, and **metamorphic**.

Igneous rocks are created when **molten** material cools and hardens. This can happen deep underground or on the surface when lava cools. Granite is a common igneous rock. It's used in buildings and kitchen countertops.

Igneous

I'm totally cool!

Sedimentary

Most sedimentary rocks are formed from small pieces of other rocks and natural materials that are laid down in layers and pressed together. The sedimentary rock limestone often contains fossils. **Fossils are only found in sedimentary rocks. . . aren't they?**

OH NO THEY **AREN'T!**

While most fossils are preserved in layers of sedimentary rocks, they've been found in metamorphic rocks, too.

Metamorphic

Metamorphic rocks started out as igneous or sedimentary rocks but have been changed by extreme heat and pressure. Only a few fossils survive this process.

Marble is a common metamorphic rock. Like granite, it's used in buildings.

Did you know that marble is a soft rock? You probably wouldn't use it for a pillow, but it's much softer than granite. The Mohs scale is a measurement of hardness that goes from 1 (softest) to 10 (hardest). A diamond scores a 10, while marble is about a 3. Granite can vary depending on the minerals it contains, but it's usually assigned a 6 or 7.

There's nothing like soft rock to help me fall asleep. . .

MAKING AN IMPRESSION

Rocks are formed by geological processes, and these processes can preserve clues to ancient life. This is called fossilization. You've probably seen fossils in museums. They're all bones that have changed into rock. . . aren't they?

OH NO THEY AREN'T!

It's true that skeletons of ancient creatures are fossilized bones, but the most common fossils are impressions (or traces) left in rock by living things.

These traces might include outlines of leaves, skin patterns, or even footprints.

Some other fossils are entire animals trapped in sticky resin that has hardened into amber over millions of years! Insects are often fossilized in amber this way.

Fossilization requires specific conditions. A living organism (or the trace it leaves behind) must be buried quickly. It can sometimes take millions of years to turn a bone or impression into a rock. The fossil will only survive if the rock isn't broken or destroyed by an earthquake, lava, or construction. The most important factor? LUCK!

Fossils can reveal a lot about ancient life, but they're pretty useless for geologists . . . aren't they?

OH NO THEY AREN'T!

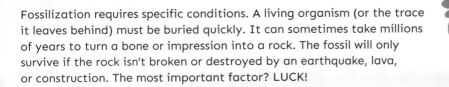

Been here long?

Geologists use fossils to date rocks. Cutting through a hillside reveals layers of rock and soil. These layers (called **strata**) often form a timeline, with the oldest layers at the bottom and the most recent at the top.

Fossils found in the same strata must have lived at roughly the same time. Their presence helps geologists tell the age of the rocks in which they were found. It helps them put together the pieces of Earth's history—a geological time scale that we divide into eons, eras, periods, epochs, and ages. For example, dinosaurs roamed the planet during the Mesozoic era, which is divided into the Triassic, Jurassic, and Cretaceous periods.

ALL THAT GLITTERS

Geology is the study of rocks and minerals—and that means it's also the study of bling. Diamonds are minerals made of pure carbon. They form in Earth's mantle, where high temperatures and pressure squeeze carbon until it forms diamond. The process can take billions of years!

When **diamonds** are found, they look like glassy pebbles. These rough diamonds need to be carefully cut and polished to make them sparkle. Talk about taking forever to get ready!

Scientists have discovered how to make **synthetic** diamonds in a lab, which only takes a few weeks. **You can tell the difference between synthetic and natural diamonds because natural diamonds are the only ones that cut glass. . . aren't they?**

OH NO THEY AREN'T!

Many materials can cut glass, including synthetic diamonds. In fact, they are just as hard as natural diamonds, and the only way to spot the real deal is to ask an expert. And by the way, a diamond *can* be damaged or destroyed through extreme pressure and heat. Despite what you might have heard, diamonds are NOT forever!

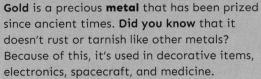

Gold is a precious **metal** that has been prized since ancient times. **Did you know** that it doesn't rust or tarnish like other metals? Because of this, it's used in decorative items, electronics, spacecraft, and medicine.

Bars of gold are worth more than bars of any other metal. . . aren't they?

OH NO THEY AREN'T!

While gold might be valuable, many metals are rarer. **Rhodium** is one of the rarest. It's used in manufacturing.

Metals like **neodymium**, **europium**, and **terbium** are far more expensive than gold—and yet they're found in almost every home! They're used to make cell phone parts.

RHODIUM

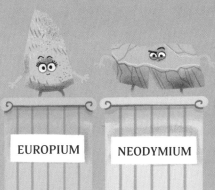

TERBIUM

EUROPIUM

NEODYMIUM

GOLD

CLIMATE SCIENCE
WEATHER OR NOT

Weather is what you experience when you walk outside. It might be sunny, rainy, windy, or snowy. Climate is the usual pattern of weather in an area over a long period of time, like the cold temperatures in the Arctic or the tropical conditions in a rainforest.

Seasonal weather changes occur as Earth moves around the Sun, leading to toastier summers and chillier winters.

And these warmer summer temperatures are caused by Earth being closer to the Sun. . . aren't they?

It's Earth's tilt that causes seasonal temperature change, not its distance from the Sun. Earth stays tilted at about the same angle as it rotates around the Sun, a bit like a spinning top! When our hemisphere tilts toward the Sun in summer, it's like holding your hand right in front of a warm fireplace.

OH NO THEY AREN'T!

Tilt-a-WORLD!

Tilt it back a bit and it's not as warm because the heat reaching your hand is no longer a direct hit. This is what Earth does, with one half tilting toward the Sun in summer and away from it in winter. The four seasons are just a cosmic tilt-a-whirl!

Weather often changes quite a bit, but climate conditions are pretty fixed. . . aren't they?

OH NO THEY AREN'T!

It was supposed to be sunny today.

Climate can be as unpredictable as the weather, just on a much grander timescale. Many factors contribute to gradual changes in climate. The flow of ocean and air currents shuffle warm and cool air around the world, which affects rainfall. Geological features such as mountain ranges play a part by blocking clouds to create deserts on one side of the mountain.

Weather is unpredictable, Dad!

Over long periods of time these factors—combined with moving tectonic plates, changes in the Sun, variations in Earth's orbit, and volcanic eruptions—can lead to extreme climate change.

PAST

PRESENT

FUTURE

TOTALLY COOL

At least five major ice ages have made Earth totally cool. The last time our planet really chilled out was around 20,000 years ago. Average temperatures were about 10°F cooler than today. Because so much water was trapped in these **glaciers**, sea levels were about 400 feet lower. That meant you could walk from Russia to Alaska—and some of our ancestors did just that!

Ice ages are caused by changes in Earth's atmosphere and orbit—and also by moving tectonic plates. **Low temperatures are the only factors needed for glaciers to form. . . aren't they?**

OH NO THEY AREN'T!

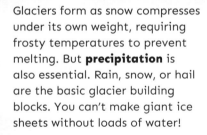

Glaciers form as snow compresses under its own weight, requiring frosty temperatures to prevent melting. But **precipitation** is also essential. Rain, snow, or hail are the basic glacier building blocks. You can't make giant ice sheets without loads of water!

Did you know that glaciers act like mirrors? They reflect the warmth of the Sun back into space, making the planet even colder!

Glaciers are as white as snow . . . aren't they?

OH NO THEY AREN'T!

Glaciers are a beautiful blue, and often shaped by **erosion** into majestic forms. In a glacier, snow is packed so tightly that any air bubbles between the flakes are squeezed out. This makes the snow form a dense crystal that reflects and scatters blue light.

The only major effects of an ice age are low temperatures and sea level changes. . . aren't they?

OH NO THEY AREN'T!

Glaciers look solid, but they flow. And as they do, they grind and scrape the land below. The Great Lakes in North America and the **fjords** in Scandinavia were both created in this way. Glaciers aren't just ice sculptures, they're ice sculptors!

HOT, HOT, HOT

The periods between ice ages are often quite a bit warmer. In fact, shortly after the Age of Dinosaurs, Earth was about 12°F warmer than it is now! This scorching interval, which lasted 200,000 years, is called the PETM. Temperatures increased rapidly for 10,000–20,000 years, and then slowly cooled off for 100,000–200,000 years. The PETM was caused by massive volcanic eruptions. Super-hot lava and ash caused the temperature spike. . . didn't they?

OH NO THEY DIDN'T!

VACATION RESORT

CLOSED
DUE TO
HEATWAVE

Looks like we got out just in time!

Erupting volcanoes release **carbon dioxide (CO_2)** and other greenhouse gases. When they're in the atmosphere, these gases trap the heat given off by Earth, causing a greenhouse effect that warms Earth. All the eruptions during the PETM meant that CO_2 levels more than doubled, making average summer temperatures at the equator soar to 106°F. If the non-flying dinosaurs hadn't already gone extinct, they would've packed their bags.

Because CO_2 makes up less than 1% of the atmosphere today, greenhouse gases are insignificant to global warming. . . aren't they?

Yuck!

OH NO THEY AREN'T!

Even tiny changes in greenhouses gas levels can raise global temperatures and increase the rate of extreme weather events such as **droughts** and storms. In the last 200 years, human activities such as burning fossil fuels have increased the level of greenhouse gases in the atmosphere by half.

Fossil fuels such as coal, oil, and natural gas are sources of **energy** formed from the remains of ancient life. They're found in layers of sedimentary rocks. **Earth constantly creates more fossil fuels, so they will always be around. . . won't they?**

OH NO THEY WON'T!

It takes millions of years for fossil fuels to form. Humans use them up faster than they're being created, making them non-renewable resources. Once they're gone, they're gone! Energy from the Sun, wind, and water won't run out, so these are **renewable energy** sources.

CH-CH-CH-CHANGES

Earth has experienced climate change again and again in its long history. Long periods of hot temperatures have given way to ice ages lasting millions of years. Rainfall, volcanic activity, and even the direction of water and air currents have also shifted through time. Sudden changes in climate are common on Earth. . . aren't they?

OH NO THEY AREN'T!

It's sure getting hot in here!

Hey humans, turn down the thermostat!

Prehistoric climate changes occurred over millions of years. But in recent times, human activity has caused changes in just decades or centuries!

The average temperature on our planet has increased by nearly 2°F in the last century. At this rate, it would take 500 years to reach the scorching climate of the PETM, which took 10,000–20,000 years through natural processes.

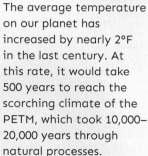

Rising global temperatures of about 2°F are small enough, though, to be unimportant. . . aren't they?

OH NO THEY AREN'T!

This small increase has already had an impact on the global climate. Glaciers are melting and sea levels are rising, and many animal and plant species are struggling to cope with the changes.

Mom!

Droughts, heat waves, and other extreme weather conditions are becoming more common. The weather in certain places might be colder at times, but the overall climate on Earth is warmer now.

We need to change the way we live in order to slow climate change. But it's too late to make these changes now. . . isn't it?

OH NO IT ISN'T!

It's not too late, but we all need to take action! There are simple things everyone can do to help, such as using less energy, recycling more, planting trees, eating less meat and dairy, and using public transport. Visit your school and local library for resources to learn more about climate change—and to find out what YOU can do.

CHEMISTRY IT'S ELEMENTAL

Chemistry is the study of matter—the stuff that our planet and everything else in the universe is made of.

The building blocks of matter are called **elements**. The smallest particle of an element is called an atom. When two or more atoms join together, they form a **molecule**. Atoms are incredibly small—it would take millions of atoms to cover a full stop.

You probably already know the names of many elements. Helium and calcium are elements. So are gold and silver. **Water and carbon dioxide are elements, too. . . aren't they?**

OH NO THEY AREN'T!

WATER (H_2O)

2 hydrogen atoms
1 oxygen atom

Mix them together!

DO NOT TRY THIS AT HOME!
Hydrogen is flammable

Water and carbon dioxide are **compounds**, with their molecules made of two or more different elements joined together. Water is made of the elements hydrogen and oxygen, while carbon and oxygen are the elements in carbon dioxide. Unique compounds form when atoms bond together in different combinations. It's a bit like cooking. Every compound has its own recipe of elemental ingredients!

The periodic table is a chart that shows all the known elements (see page 56–57). Each element is represented by a symbol of one or two letters. The symbol for oxygen is O. Carbon is C. Not all of the symbols are so straightforward, though.

Can you guess the chemical symbol for gold? It's not G, but Au! The symbol comes from the Latin word for gold, Aurum. Maybe it should be Bl for bling. . .

All elements on the periodic table are found naturally on Earth. . . aren't they?

| 6 C | 8 O |

| 79 Au |

OH NO THEY AREN'T!

I'm a "glass half full" kind of guy.

There are 24 synthetic elements. They were created by scientists using special equipment and are extremely rare. The most common natural element on Earth is oxygen. Number two is silicon.

Did you know that oxygen and silicon are the main ingredients of sand, which is used to make glass?

CHAIN REACTION

Matter exists in four basic states: solid, liquid, gas, and plasma.

In a **solid**, such as a rock, the particles (either atoms or molecules) are tightly packed together and arranged in a regular way, so the solid holds its shape.

The particles of a **liquid** such as water are more loosely packed and can move around. That means liquids don't have their own shape—they flow and take the shape of whatever container holds them.

These molecules are mmm good!

The particles in a **gas** are all free to move around on their own. Oxygen and helium are gases at room temperature.

Plasma is like a gas where extra energy (usually heat) has pulled its particles apart. Stars are made of plasma, making it the most common state of matter in the universe!

States of matter don't change. They're constant. . . aren't they?

OH NO THEY AREN'T!

Changes in pressure and temperature transform matter from solids to liquids to gases—and back again! Water is the liquid form of the compound H_2O (two molecules of hydrogen and one of oxygen). If you lower the temperature, liquid water turns into a solid: ice! If you heat ice, it melts into a liquid. Continue heating the liquid water and it'll become a gas called steam.

Water's transformations into different states of matter are caused by chemical reactions. . . aren't they?

OH NO THEY AREN'T!

When liquid water freezes into solid ice, it's still water, just in a different form. This is called a **physical change**. A chemical change is different—substances combine with each other to create something completely new, and this change can't usually be reversed. For example, when iron is exposed to oxygen and water, they react with each other to create a completely different compound called rust, or iron oxide.

From frozen to fluid!

PHYSICS
FORCE OF ATTRACTION

Some physics is the study of attraction—not the attraction celebrated on Valentine's Day, but the forces that hold our universe together. For example, the force that holds atoms together in a molecule is called the electromagnetic force. The particles that make up a solid are also bound together by electromagnetic forces. Weaker versions of the same force result in liquids and gases. Electromagnetic forces are all about attraction. . . aren't they?

I can't help being so attractive!

OH NO THEY AREN'T!

They're also about repulsion, or pushing away. Atoms are made up of smaller particles, many of which have either positive or negative charges. Two positive charges repel each other, and so do two negative charges. But a positive and a negative charge attract each other. In physics, opposites literally attract!

You can see this in action with magnets, which have a positive and a negative pole. When the north poles of two magnets are placed together, they push each other away. But place a north pole near a south pole, and the magnets are attracted to each other.

Electromagnetic forces are the only forces that affect matter in our universe. . . aren't they?

OH NO THEY AREN'T!

Gravity is another important attractive force. It keeps the planets in our solar system orbiting around the Sun. It also causes objects to fall to the ground when they're dropped or thrown.

Planets that gravitate together, stick together!

Gravity must be the strongest attractive force in the universe. . . isn't it?

OH NO IT ISN'T!

Gravity, I'm falling for you!

Gravity is actually the weakest force. It's most effective at great distances, and it can be overcome—such as when astronauts fly into space. The electromagnetic force that binds many particles together is by far the stronger of the two

HIGH ENERGY

Anything and everything in our universe is a form of matter. . . isn't it?

OH NO IT ISN'T!

The universe contains many things that aren't matter. One of these is energy. Energy is often defined as the ability to do work, and it's what makes objects move or heat up. We can't create energy, and we can't destroy it either. But it comes in different forms, and it can be converted from one form to another, such as wind turbines turning the movement energy of wind into electrical energy.

The different forms of energy can be grouped into two main types: kinetic and potential.

Potential energy is the energy stored in an object, like a bicycle parked at the top of a hill or a fully charged battery.

Kinetic energy is the energy of objects in motion, such as a rolling ball or a falling apple.

Ooh, ooh, ah, ah!

Did you know that **light** is a form of energy? Sunlight travels to Earth, and plants capture this energy. They convert it into a store of chemical energy that they use to grow. Solar panels capture sunlight too, but they convert it into electrical energy. The Sun also provides another form of energy that's super important for all life: **heat**.

We can see some forms of energy, like light. There are others, such as heat, that we primarily feel. We can't hear energy, though. All forms of energy are silent. . . aren't they?

Sound is a type of energy! Like light, sound energy also travels in waves. Our ears convert sound waves into conversations, honking horns, and every other noise we hear. When you tap your feet to the beat of a catchy tune, you're grooving to an energetic wave!

OH NO THEY AREN'T!

HONK!

ENGINEERING EVERYWHERE

Engineering is everywhere. This book was printed with ink developed by an engineer. The chair you're sitting on was also designed with the help of engineers! Through the use of science and math, engineering is the process of designing and maintaining products and systems. All it takes to be an engineer is excellent math skills. . . isn't it?

OH NO IT ISN'T!

Mathematics is definitely a key part of engineering, but understanding **scientific principles** is just as important, and so are creativity and communication skills.

There are many specialties in engineering. All of them are about fixing broken things. . . aren't they?

OH NO THEY AREN'T!

Many engineers are inventors. They don't just repair broken products and systems, they also create them!

Can someone fix this for me? I'm no engineer!

ERROR!

Here are four of the largest engineering fields:

Civil engineering is about designing structures from buildings and bridges to canals and colosseums, as well as monuments like the Eiffel Tower.

Electrical engineers are experts on the electrical systems that power machines. They often work very closely with mechanical engineers.

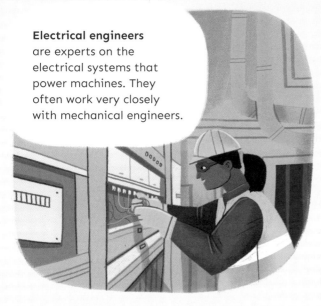

Mechanical engineering focuses on machines—including robots, roller coasters, and refrigerators!

Chemical engineers transform raw materials into useful items. Shampoo, ice cream, and toilet paper are all products developed by chemical engineers.

Some engineering fields focus on specific industries or specialties of science. Computer engineers design computers and networks. Biomedical engineering improves health and medical systems. Designing aircraft and spacecraft is the realm of aerospace engineering.

Got a problem? Engineering has a solution!

MONUMENTAL MARVELS

Some of the greatest feats of engineering are world-famous landmarks. The Great Wall of China was constructed over a period of more than 2,000 years. It was primarily made for defense, but also helped to control trade and the movement of people across the border. The wall was engineered to serve all of these purposes while twisting around a landscape of hills, valleys, and rivers. The oldest sections of the wall were made from earth. Once builders started using fired bricks instead, construction went faster and the walls became stronger.

Did you know that parts of the Great Wall are held together by soup? A sticky rice porridge was mixed with a chemical called slaked lime, made by mixing lime with water, to create a cement-like **mortar**. Who knew an old recipe for sticky rice porridge could be an engineering marvel?

Good enough to eat!

The Great Wall of China is the largest human-made structure ever. Its many sections are visible from space. . . aren't they?

OH NO THEY AREN'T!

The Great Wall of China cannot usually be seen from far out in space—at least, not without cameras with powerful zoom lenses or superhero vision.

The **Golden Gate Bridge** is a modern engineering marvel that spans a 1-mile opening to the San Francisco Bay.

Civil engineers designed the Golden Gate Bridge as a suspension bridge. This means the weight of the deck, where cars and people move across, is suspended from cables that support it. When it was completed in 1937, the Golden Gate Bridge was the longest suspension bridge in the world.

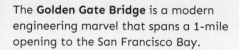

> Neither the longest bridge, nor golden!

In 2022, the **1915 Çanakkale Bridge** in Turkey overtook it to become the world's longest bridge.

Did you know that there are seven main types of bridges? That's seven different solutions for carrying people over obstacles. . . all devised by civil engineers!

Truss

Arch

Cantilever

Tied Arch

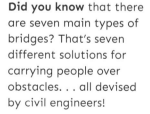

Beam

Suspension

Cable-stayed

CHOCOLATE FACTORY

Many varieties of food have been perfected through chemical engineering. Using chemistry, engineers invent new types of foods, drinks, and flavors, as well as the processes that transform raw ingredients into our favorite meals and keep them fresh.

It takes a combination of chemical reactions to turn pods from the cacao plant into a delicious chocolaty treat. The seeds (or "beans") inside pods go through a process called **fermentation** that helps to develop a richer chocolate flavor. They are then dried, roasted, and ground up. Then the ground-up beans are processed even further and mixed with a variety of ingredients to create different types of chocolate.

Chemical engineers manage every chocolaty step in the process to control the flavor, smell, color, and consistency. For example, shortening the fermentation time makes the chocolate more bitter, while increasing the amount of cocoa butter or fat in the mixture makes it creamier.

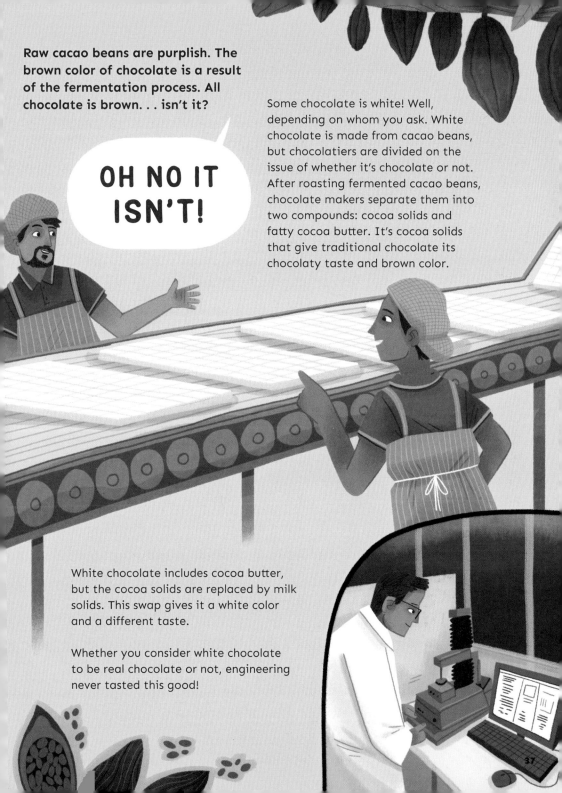

Raw cacao beans are purplish. The brown color of chocolate is a result of the fermentation process. All chocolate is brown. . . isn't it?

OH NO IT ISN'T!

Some chocolate is white! Well, depending on whom you ask. White chocolate is made from cacao beans, but chocolatiers are divided on the issue of whether it's chocolate or not. After roasting fermented cacao beans, chocolate makers separate them into two compounds: cocoa solids and fatty cocoa butter. It's cocoa solids that give traditional chocolate its chocolaty taste and brown color.

White chocolate includes cocoa butter, but the cocoa solids are replaced by milk solids. This swap gives it a white color and a different taste.

Whether you consider white chocolate to be real chocolate or not, engineering never tasted this good!

37

PLANET PROTECTORS

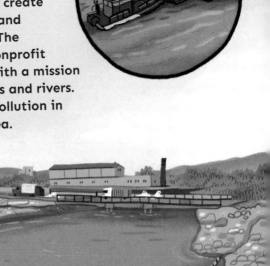

Environmental engineers use science to create cleaner, safer products while restoring and preserving our planet and its systems. The Ocean Cleanup is a good example: a nonprofit environmental engineering company with a mission to remove plastic pollution from oceans and rivers. They've created machines that catch pollution in rivers, stopping it from reaching the sea.

Differences in tides, currents, and wildlife—as well as the shape of each river—mean that engineers must customize the barriers to suit each river. But the engineering doesn't stop there! The company also engineers systems and processes to sustainably reuse the plastic they collect, such as making it into useful products like sunglasses.

Environmental engineers are only focused on cleaning up. . . aren't they?

OH NO THEY AREN'T!

Environmental engineers also find solutions for building healthier, more **sustainable** communities, slowing climate change, and allowing humans to coexist with nature. They're planet protectors!

Environmental engineers and scientists created an archipelago, or chain of islands, in the middle of Lake Markermeer in the Netherlands. They did this to revive the lake, which had declined due to human activity.

Engineers constructed the islands—called the **Marker Wadden**—by designing walls of sand and filling the spaces between them with mud.

LITTLE GREBE

MARKER WADDEN

COMMON SHELDUCK

BLACK-HEADED GULL

Wildlife appeared almost immediately! Soon birds were nesting on the islands, plant life returned, and fish spawned (laid eggs) in the shallows. The **ecosystem** of the entire lake improved!

Engineers are still hard at work at the Marker Wadden to balance the ecosystem. They are studying tides and weather patterns to keep erosion from washing away the archipelago. No matter how clever the solution, environmental engineering is still at the mercy of natural forces.

39

ASTRONOMY OUT OF THIS WORLD

Astronomy is the study of everything in the universe beyond Earth's atmosphere. Earth is just one of many objects in a solar system with our star, the Sun, at its center. There are other planets as well as moons, asteroids, and comets. But our star is just one of billions in our galaxy, and the universe contains billions or even trillions of other galaxies. That makes astronomy a very big subject! Stars like the Sun are balls of fire. . . aren't they?

OH NO THEY AREN'T!

There's no fire on the Sun. It's a ball of super-heated gas, a result of the **nuclear fusion** taking place in its core. In this process, hydrogen atoms smash together to make helium. The intense energy released creates heat and light, which makes the Sun glow.

The planet closest to the Sun is the hottest. . . isn't it?

OH NO IT ISN'T!

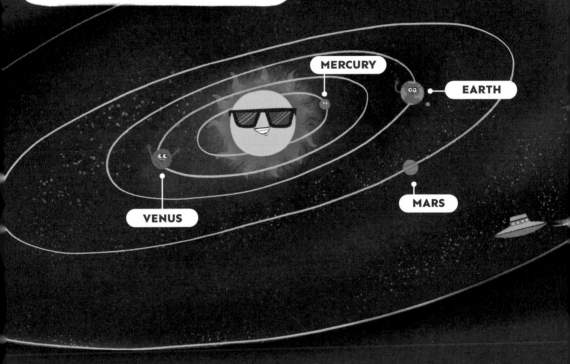

MERCURY

EARTH

VENUS

MARS

Mercury is the closest planet to the Sun, but it's actually cooler than the next closest planet, Venus! Venus's atmosphere is mainly carbon dioxide, which traps the Sun's heat and keeps it nice and toasty. Mercury hardly has any atmosphere, so although it can reach temperatures close to Venus's during the day, at night it loses all that heat and can plunge to -290°F!

Earth maintains a pleasant average temperature of 59°F, while the farthest planet, Neptune, is a frigid -330°F!

Did you know that Pluto used to be considered the ninth planet? It was demoted to a **dwarf planet** in 2006 after astronomers discovered several similar-sized bodies in a region of icy objects called the **Kuiper Belt**. Poor little Pluto.

I'll go play with the other dwarf planets then. . .

MANY MOONS

Natural satellites known as moons orbit many of the planets. Dwarf planets like Pluto can also have moons, and so can asteroids! According to NASA, there are currently more than 290 moons orbiting the eight planets of our solar system.

The Earth's moon is called, well. . . the Moon. It plays an important part in our everyday lives. Its gravitational pull creates tides in the oceans. But its gravity is weaker than Earth's, because the Moon itself is a lot smaller than Earth—only about a quarter as wide. **All moons are smaller than planets. . . aren't they?**

OH NO THEY AREN'T!

In the left corner we have Ganymede, moon of Jupiter.

Mercury is the smallest planet, and our Moon is even smaller, but the largest moon in the solar system, Ganymede, beats Mercury in a size contest. Ganymede orbits Jupiter. Saturn's largest moon, Titan, is also bigger than Mercury.

In the right corner we have Mercury, smallest planet in our solar system.

Unlike planets, natural satellites are devoid of any atmosphere. . . aren't they?

OH NO THEY AREN'T!

Or at least, not all of them. Saturn's Titan is the only moon with a thick atmosphere, but several other moons in our solar system have thinner ones. Even the Moon has an atmosphere. It's extremely thin, like the atmosphere on Mercury. This kind of thin atmosphere is called an **exosphere** and it doesn't provide much protection from the Sun's **radiation** like Earth's thick atmosphere does.

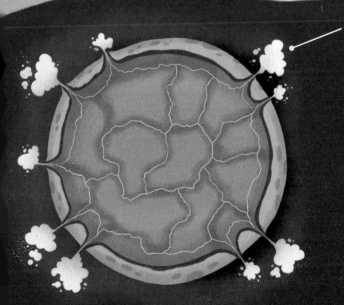

IO

Did you know that some moons have oceans deep beneath their surfaces? Others have volcanic activity, such as Io, a moon of Jupiter that is covered in erupting volcanoes!

Don't tell the demoted dwarf planet Pluto, but some moons are like little planets. They might even contain evidence of microscopic life!

BLACK HOLES

Black holes form in space, often when a massive star runs out of fuel, then collapses on itself. The resulting explosion, called a supernova, is of celestial proportions! What's left after the explosion is a black hole: a point where gravity is so strong that even light can't escape it! This is why they are black. Black holes are cosmic vacuum cleaners that suck in everything... aren't they?

We're REALLY not in Kansas anymore!

OH NO THEY AREN'T!

Black holes don't suck in objects like a vacuum cleaner, but they do tug objects into them if they get too close. Objects fall into the "hole" because of the enormous pull of gravity inside. Black holes sit at the center of most large galaxies, including our own Milky Way. At the edge of a black hole, the material swirling around and falling inside heats up and creates enormous forces. These forces produce powerful twisting magnetic fields, which may shoot out jets of material (gas and dust) at near the speed of light. This isn't a feature you'd want in a vacuum cleaner!

The first black hole photographed was at the center of a galaxy called M87. It was captured by a network of radio telescopes called the Event Horizon Telescope. The photograph confirmed that black holes are holes in space. . . aren't they?

OH NO THEY AREN'T!

Black holes look like holes, but they aren't empty. At the very center of a black hole is the **singularity**, a point where dense concentrations of matter are squeezed into a very tiny space. Within this infinitely small point, time and space don't exist!

Does this mean I'll never be late inside a black hole?

You'll also never be on time!

Don't worry if this is totally baffling. Getting your head around a black hole is as hard as trying to escape one! Scientists even struggle to understand them.

LIFE ON MARS

The search for extraterrestrial life has captivated generations of astronomers. Our galaxy contains billions of planets. Is Earth the only one with intelligent life? Astronomers have searched for clues, and in the 19th century, one observed channels on Mars. These structures were evidence of Martians. . . weren't they?

OH NO THEY WEREN'T!

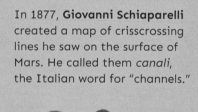

Giovanni Schiaparelli

In 1877, **Giovanni Schiaparelli** created a map of crisscrossing lines he saw on the surface of Mars. He called them *canali*, the Italian word for "channels."

The American astronomer **Percival Lowell** later interpreted them as canals made by a Martian civilization. Most astronomers disagreed, but the public became obsessed. Stories and music were written about the aliens, and when one story called *The War of the Worlds* was broadcast on the radio, it convinced people that Martians really were invading Earth!

When the spacecraft *Mariner 4* flew by Mars in 1965, it took photographs of the planet and proved that there were no canals. . . and no canal-building Martians.

The only life in the universe is on Earth. Scientists are certain of this. . . aren't they?

OH NO THEY AREN'T!

Haha, the humans will never find us!

The **SETI Institute** is a nonprofit science organization that searches for extraterrestrial life. Using high-powered telescopes, astronomers look for radio signals that might have been sent by an alien civilization. Of the millions of signals collected every hour, most come from human activity. We're a noisy bunch! These have to be discarded before the most promising signals can be investigated further.

Is anybody out there?

Astronomers have also been involved in *sending* messages to aliens. So far, no alien messages have been detected, and none of our messages have ever been answered. That's ghosting of cosmic proportions!

DIGITAL TECHNOLOGY
CONNECTED COMPUTERS

Digital technology is the term used for the whole collection of electronic tools we use to create, access, store, and process data. Cell phones and computers transmit data in the form of text, audio, and even video. We use GPS technology to access location data to meet up with friends. Digital technology probably woke you up this morning!

GO STRAIGHT AHEAD

One more computer and we'll have no office space at all!

Did you know that early computers from the 1950s were big enough to fill an entire room? They were called mainframes and were extremely expensive—only wealthy businesses and governments could afford to use them.

Digital technology wouldn't become widely available to the general public until the 1980s, when personal computers became affordable. The launch of the **World Wide Web** in 1991 and the debut of the first smartphone in 1994 made our world truly digital.

The World Wide Web and the Internet are the same thing. . . aren't they?

OH NO THEY AREN'T!

The World Wide Web, or "the web," refers to the web pages we browse. The Internet is the network of connected computers and servers that holds the web pages—like the roads that connect towns and cities together. If the Internet is a giant library, the World Wide Web is the books inside it. But there's much more to the Internet than just the web.

Most online gaming platforms are hosted on Internet servers, not the web. Digital devices like security cameras use the Internet to access and transmit data. Email services have web pages to make them easier for us to use, but electronic mail itself is often sent though the Internet. That digital message you wish you didn't send? It's been delivered. . . via the Internet.

TOUCHSCREEN TELEPHONES

The first call ever made from a handheld cell phone happened on April 3, 1973. The phone was invented by engineer Marty Cooper, and it was nicknamed "the brick"—because it was about the size and weight of a brick! You couldn't slip this heavy phone into your pocket or do anything with it except make phone calls. . . or maybe use it as a paperweight.

Marty Cooper

Still the original cell phone!

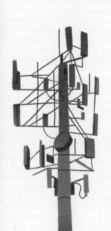

Cell phones (also known as mobile, handy, or hand phones) are so called because conversations and data is transmitted through a network of smaller areas called cells.

Today's phone networks are digital and global and are called the Global System for Mobile Communications—or GSM for short. GSM is what the G stands for in the network speeds such as 5G. The higher the number, the faster, better, and more reliably the data moves through the network, resulting in better sound. . . and higher quality streaming for all those cat videos.

Cell phones have come a long way since that original "brick." They're portable computers now! Old-school phones had buttons to push, but modern phones feature touchscreen technology. The harder you tap, the more responsive the phones are. . . aren't they?

OH NO THEY AREN'T!

The touchscreen on a phone is **capacitive**. This means it detects the change in its electrical field when your finger touches the screen and conducts some of the charge.

Tapping or swiping the screen triggers the phone's **programming**, but it doesn't matter how hard you press, only where and how often you touch the screen.

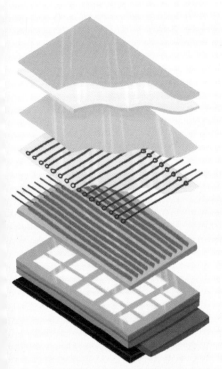

Why can't I catch these mice?!

A touchscreen won't respond if you wear gloves because they block the transmission of electricity to your finger. Cats can play games on a touchscreen device because, like human hands, their paws conduct electricity!

AI

AI stands for artificial intelligence—the ability of a computer to learn and adapt in a similar way to a human brain. AI has become a key component of everyday digital products. It checks for spelling errors in emails and powers suggestions from websites and streaming platforms, to serve more cat videos than you ever wanted to watch.

The concept of artificial intelligence and its uses are very recent. . . aren't they?

OH NO THEY AREN'T!

John McCarthy

Scientists have been working on artificial intelligence for over 50 years—and theorizing about it for centuries! The term was first coined by computer scientist **John McCarthy** in 1955. It wasn't until the 21st century that developments in AI would really speed up, and humans would carry AI in their pockets!

AI-enabled devices like cell phones are able to think just like humans. . . aren't they?

OH NO THEY AREN'T!

You're not as smart as you think you are. . .

AI can combine existing knowledge in unique ways, but it doesn't think the way we do. Artificial intelligence is restricted by the data it is given and by **algorithms**, the step-by-step sets of commands it must obey.

Following these algorithms, AI can analyze huge amounts of data at superhuman speeds. It can pick out patterns the human eye can't perceive. But AI doesn't have self-awareness or emotions—yet. These qualities deeply enhance the way humans think, but may be part of AI programs in the future.

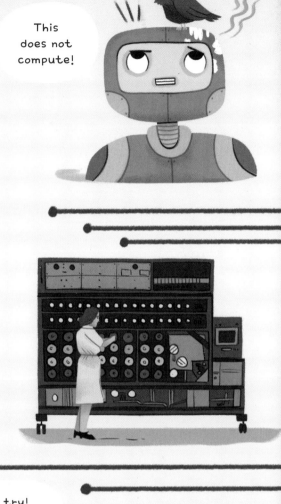

This does not compute!

Alan Turing

In 1950, researcher **Alan Turing** created a thought experiment that could reveal if a computer showed intelligence that couldn't be distinguished from human intelligence. He called it the "imitation game," but we now call it the Turing test in his honor.

Nice try! You can't fool me.

Do you think a computer could fool you into thinking it was a real person?

ROBOTICS

Robots are machines engineered to perform tasks automatically. They're all designed to look like humans. . . aren't they?

OH NO THEY AREN'T!

A robot is run by a computer that acts like its brain and contains the programming that tells the robot what to do.

A third of the world's robots are arm-like machines found in factories where they make cars. Hospitals, laboratories, and factories also use robots to perform a range of dangerous and repetitive tasks.

Did you know that astronauts operate robots to perform experiments and repairs in space?

Engineers can train robots to make a TV, move hazardous chemicals, or even dance by guiding them through every step and movement. The robot's computer memorizes and repeats the patterns. **Autonomous** robots are programmed to work out solutions on their own!

Robots are new, digital innovations. . . aren't they?

OH NO THEY AREN'T!

One of the first robots ever created was made by an Ancient Greek scientist named Archytas. It was a wooden pigeon that could fly about 650 feet, powered by steam.

Archytas

George Devol

Unimate was the first programmable robot—a robotic arm invented by George Devol in the 1950s and used on assembly lines to weld car parts. A smaller version of the robot arm was engineered to pour coffee!

Unlike Unimate, some modern robots can move around. Many have AI in their programming to help them learn faster. Self-driving cars are robots. So are some

types of drones. Cobots or collaborative robots are among the newest robots. They're designed specifically to work safely with humans. In the not-so-distant future, your first job by might be working with cobot co-workers!

THE PERIODIC TABLE

The periodic table is an ingenious system for organizing the elements. It was created by the Russian chemist Dmitri Mendeleev.

Group

| 1 | 2 | 3 | 4 | 5 | 6 | 7 | 8 | 9 |

Period

The letters are symbols that represent an element's name.

1 **H**

Above them are atomic numbers, which represent the number of protons in each atom of a particular element.

Period									
1	1 H								
2	3 Li	4 Be							
3	11 Na	12 Mg							
4	19 K	20 Ca	21 Sc	22 Ti	23 V	24 Cr	25 Mn	26 Fe	27 Co
5	37 Rb	38 Sr	39 Y	40 Zr	41 Nb	42 Mo	43 Tc	44 Ru	45 Rh
6	55 Cs	56 Ba	57 La	72 Hf	73 Ta	74 W	75 Re	76 Os	77 Ir
7	87 Fr	88 Ra	89 Ac	104 Rf	105 Db	106 Sg	107 Bh	108 Hs	109 Mt

Cerium

58 Ce	59 Pr	60 Nd	61 Pm	62 Sm	63 Eu
90 Th	91 Pa	92 U	93 Np	94 Pu	95 Am

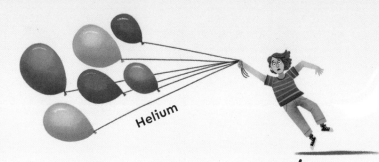

Helium

								2 **He**
			5 **B**	6 **C**	7 **N**	8 **O**	9 **F**	10 **Ne**
			13 **Al**	14 **Si**	15 **P**	16 **S**	17 **Cl**	18 **Ar**
28 **Ni**	29 **Cu**	30 **Zn**	31 **Ga**	32 **Ge**	33 **As**	34 **Se**	35 **Br**	36 **Kr**
46 **Pd**	47 **Ag**	48 **Cd**	49 **In**	50 **Sn**	51 **Sb**	52 **Te**	53 **I**	54 **Xe**
78 **Pt**	79 **Au**	80 **Hg**	81 **Ti**	82 **Pb**	83 **Bi**	84 **Po**	85 **At**	86 **Rn**
110 **Ds**	111 **Rg**	112 **Cn**	113 **Nh**	114 **Fl**	115 **Mc**	116 **Lv**	117 **Ts**	118 **Og**

Copper

64 **Gd**	65 **Tb**	66 **Dy**	67 **Ho**	68 **Er**	69 **Tm**	70 **Yb**	71 **Lu**
96 **Cm**	97 **Bk**	98 **Cf**	99 **Es**	100 **Fm**	101 **Md**	102 **No**	103 **Lr**

MAP OF THE SOLAR SYSTEM

This is a map of our solar system, showing the eight planets in the order that they orbit the Sun.

MOON

VENUS

EARTH

MARS

ASTEROID BELT

JUPITER

MERCURY

SUN

In reality, the size differences between the planets are more extreme—if Jupiter were the size of a watermelon, then Earth would only be about the size of a cherry tomato!

The gaps between the planets are much bigger too, and they each travel around the Sun at their own pace rather than sitting in a neat line.

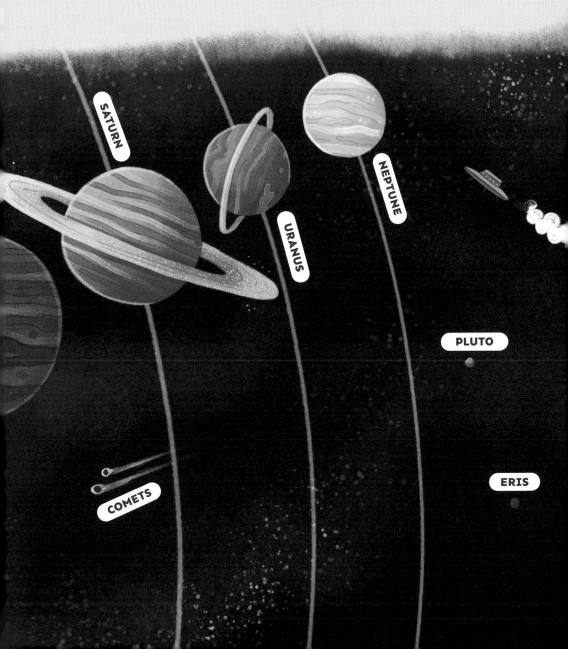

SATURN

URANUS

NEPTUNE

PLUTO

ERIS

COMETS

GLOSSARY

algorithm a series of step-by-step instructions for completing a task or solving a problem; often part of a computer's programming

atmosphere a layer of gases that often surrounds a planet or other body in space

atom the smallest particle of an element that can exist; these particles are the basic building blocks of matter

autonomous something that can work or move by itself

capacitive able to collect and store an electrical charge

carbon dioxide (CO₂) a greenhouse gas made up of carbon and oxygen, which builds up in the atmosphere and traps Earth's heat

chemical reaction a change that takes place when matter transforms from one substance into another

compound a substance made of two or more elements that are bonded together

core the extremely hot center of Earth; the core is divided into a solid inner section surrounded by a liquid outer part

crust the thin, outermost layer of Earth, which forms the rocky surface where we live

drought a long period of time when there's not enough rain

dwarf planet a spherical object that orbits the Sun without a clear path and is too small to be considered a planet

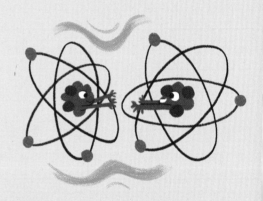

ecosystem a community of living things and the environment around them

element a substance made up of only one type of atom and which cannot be broken down into a simpler substance

energy the ability to do work; energy is needed to move or change things

erosion the carrying away of small pieces of rock and soil by wind, water, or ice, after they have been worn away by weathering

exosphere the outermost layer of a thick atmosphere where the gases are spread very thin; some planets and moons have only a thin exosphere

extraterrestrial coming from somewhere in the universe other than Earth

fermentation a chemical reaction used in food production that converts sugars into alcohol or acids

fjord a deep, narrow coastal valley carved out by a glacier and then filled with seawater

fossil fuel a source of energy, such as coal, oil, or natural gas, that is made from the remains of long-dead animals and plants

glacier a very large, slow-moving mass of ice that forms over many years from layers of compressed snow

gravity a force that pulls matter towards each other

Kuiper Belt a ring-shaped area of icy objects located beyond the orbit of Neptune, which includes Pluto and several other dwarf planets

mantle the middle section of Earth, located between the crust and the core

metal a type of hard substance that conducts heat and electricity well and can be hammered into thin sheets

microscopic something very small that can only be seen with a magnifying tool called a "microscope"

Milky Way the galaxy that includes our Sun and solar system, as well as billions of other stars and smaller objects

mineral a naturally occurring solid made of non-living materials, which has a regular crystalline structure

molecule the smallest possible unit of a chemical compound, which includes two or more atoms held together by chemical bonds

molten something melted into a super-hot liquid like lava

mortar a material made to hold bricks or stones together in construction

nuclear fusion the process in which the nuclei (centers) of two atoms smash together and combine, releasing energy as they do

physical change a change in the physical form of a substance, for example, from a solid to a liquid

precipitation water that falls from clouds in various forms, for example as rain and snow

programming creating a list of set instructions to tell a computer what to do

radiation energy in motion; waves of energy that travel through space

renewable energy power from natural sources, such as the Sun or wind, which will not run out or harm the planet

satellite any object that orbits another; satellites can be natural, such as moons, or artificial, such as the spacecraft we send into orbit

server a computer that keeps and sends information to other computers

singularity a tiny point in space-time with infinite mass and gravity so strong that the normal rules of physics break down

solar system all of the objects held in orbit by the gravity of our Sun, including planets, moons, and asteroids

strata layers of rock

supernova the explosion that happens when a star several times larger than the Sun uses up its fuel and collapses in on itself

sustainable using resources in a way that doesn't harm the environment and helps to protect it in the future

synthetic a material made by people rather than from items found in nature

tectonic plates large sections of Earth's crust that move slowly around

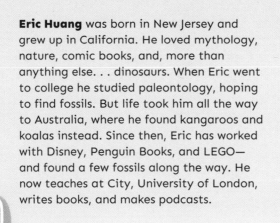

Eric Huang was born in New Jersey and grew up in California. He loved mythology, nature, comic books, and, more than anything else. . . dinosaurs. When Eric went to college he studied paleontology, hoping to find fossils. But life took him all the way to Australia, where he found kangaroos and koalas instead. Since then, Eric has worked with Disney, Penguin Books, and LEGO— and found a few fossils along the way. He now teaches at City, University of London, writes books, and makes podcasts.

ABOUT THE AUTHOR

Acknowledgements

Thank you to Holly, Alice, and Nancy for all of your invaluable feedback. Thank you Shannon for signing up this series. And thanks to Angela, Brian, Elias, Emma, Lynsey, Nic, and my mom for pushing me to write!

Eric Huang

Acknowledgements

A big thanks to Kat and Sarah for all of the fantastic design work and steering of the ship on this series. Thank you also Doreen, Kate, and Tom for the opportunity and continued support.

Sam Caldwell

ABOUT THE ILLUSTRATOR

Sam Caldwell is an illustrator based in Glasgow where he lives with his wife and two cats: Tonks and Luna. Sam loves inventing characters and creating images packed full of detail, texture, and color. He is passionate about animals and nature, and when he's not drawing, Sam can often be found exploring the Scottish Highlands. He has illustrated many books for children, including the award-winning *Do Bears Poop In The Woods?*